Working Horses

Race Horses

by Rachel Grack

Bullfrog Books

Ideas for Parents and Teachers

Bullfrog Books let children practice reading informational text at the earliest reading levels. Repetition, familiar words, and photo labels support early readers.

Before Reading

- Discuss the cover photo. What does it tell them?

- Look at the picture glossary together. Read and discuss the words.

Read the Book

- "Walk" through the book and look at the photos. Let the child ask questions. Point out the photo labels.

- Read the book to the child, or have him or her read independently.

After Reading

- Prompt the child to think more. Ask: There are many kinds of horse races. Have you ever seen one? Would you like to?

Bullfrog Books are published by Jump!
5357 Penn Avenue South
Minneapolis, MN 55419
www.jumplibrary.com

Library of Congress Cataloging-in-Publication Data

Names: Koestler-Grack, Rachel A., 1973– author.
Title: Race horses / by Rachel Grack.
Description: Minneapolis, MN: Jump!, Inc., [2024]
Series: Working horses | Includes index.
Audience: Ages 5–8
Identifiers: LCCN 2022051867 (print)
LCCN 2022051868 (ebook)
ISBN 9798885244992 (hardcover)
ISBN 9798885245005 (paperback)
ISBN 9798885245012 (ebook)
Subjects: LCSH: Race horses—Juvenile literature.
Horse racing—Juvenile literature.
Classification: LCC SF335.6 .K64 2024 (print)
LCC SF335.6 (ebook)
DDC 798.4—dc23/eng/20221104
LC record available at https://lccn.loc.gov/2022051867
LC ebook record available at https://lccn.loc.gov/2022051868

Editor: Katie Chanez
Designer: Molly Ballanger

Photo Credits: Cheryl Ann Quigley/Shutterstock, cover; Hans Christiansson/Shutterstock, 1, 22bm; Margo Harrison/Shutterstock, 3, 22tm; Lo Chun Kit/Getty, 4, 16, 18–19, 23tm, 23tr; Ryan Hoel/Dreamstime, 5; R. Wellen Photography/Shutterstock, 6–7, 23bm; Mick Atkins/Shutterstock, 8–9; Kertu Saarits/Dreamstime, 10–11, 22bl; Pieter Sorber WorldRC/Shutterstock, 12, 13, 22tr, 23br; Sergei Bachlakov/Shutterstock, 14–15, 23bl; Mikhail Pogosov/Shutterstock, 17, 23tl; Joe Hendrickson/Alamy, 20–21; Delmas Lehman/Shutterstock, 22tl; ID1974/Shutterstock, 22br; dikkenss/Shutterstock, 24.

Printed in the United States of America at Corporate Graphics in North Mankato, Minnesota.

Table of Contents

At the Track

trainer

This horse trains.

Why?

It will race!

Lucky learns to run on a track.

track

Horses have long legs.
They take big strides.

Race horses are strong.
Some jump over fences.

These horses race many miles.

They might not go fast.

But they keep going!

Blaze pulls a sulky.

sulky

A driver rides in the sulky.
They race to the finish line.

driver

barrel

Flash races at a rodeo.
She runs around barrels.
The fastest horse wins!

Jockeys race horses.

jockey

gate

They wait behind the gates.

They are off!

The horses run around the track.

They run a lap.

They race to the finish line!

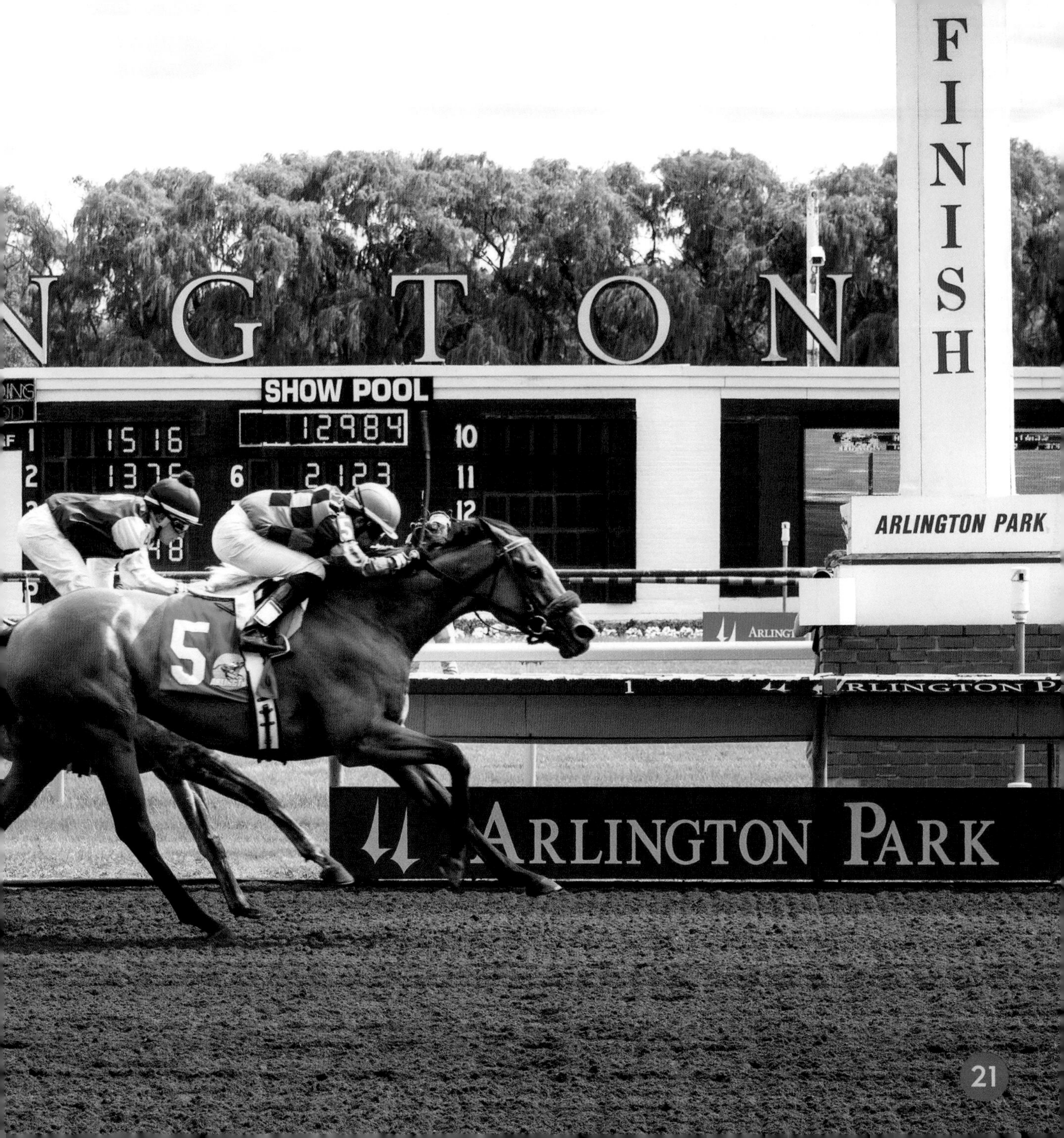
FINISH
NGTON
SHOW POOL
ARLINGTON PARK
ARLINGTON PARK

On the Job

There are many kinds of horse races. Take a look at some!

barrel races
Horses race around barrels.

jump races
Horses race while jumping over fences and other obstacles.

harness races
Horses race while pulling carts and drivers.

endurance races
Horses race many miles over many days.

flat races
Horses race on a flat track.

quarter horse races
Horses race for one quarter of a mile.

Picture Glossary

gates
Doors used to make sure race horses start at the same time.

jockeys
Professional riders in horse races.

lap
One complete trip around a track.

rodeo
A contest in which riders compete in different events.

strides
Long steps.

sulky
A two-wheeled cart used in some horse races.

Index

To Learn More

Finding more information is as easy as 1, 2, 3.

❶ Go to www.factsurfer.com

❷ Enter "racehorses" into the search box.

❸ Choose your book to see a list of websites.